TWEETABLE
BARACK OBAMA

Infotainment Press

TWEETABLE
BARACK OBAMA

QUIPS, QUOTES & OTHER ONE-LINERS

We learned that no union founded on the principles of liberty and equality could survive half-slave and half-free.

* * *

The American people . . . deserve a government that is truly of, by, and for the people.

* * *

Our nation is at war against a far-reaching network of violence and hatred.

* * *

Progress is essential to peace.

We do not have to think that human nature is perfect for us to still believe that the human condition can be perfected.

☀

I understand why war is not popular, but I also know this: The belief that peace is desirable is rarely enough to achieve it.

☀

For human rights to reach those who suffer the boot of oppression, we need your voices to speak out.

☀

I have never been more hopeful about America.

The Freedom of Information Act is perhaps the most powerful instrument we have for making . . . government honest and transparent.

❀

We believe that when [universal human rights] are respected, nations are more successful and our world is safer and more just.

❀

All people yearn for certain things: . . . the freedom to live as you choose.

❀

It is easier to blame others than to look inward.

I believe that it is important for us to set aside some of the gamesmanship in this town and get something done.

✦

W hen our interests and values are at stake, we have a responsibility to act.

✦

I n the 21st century, capable, reliable, and transparent institutions are the key to success.

✦

N o country is going to create wealth if its leaders exploit the economy to enrich themselves.

*T*o protect the freedom of all the voters, those in power must accept constraints.

✡

*P*reserving our individual freedoms ultimately requires collective action.

✡

*T*hreatening Israel with destruction or repeating vile stereotypes about Jews is deeply wrong.

✡

*D*on't shortchange the future, because of fear in the present.

*N*one of us are fully free when others in the human family remain shackled by poverty or disease or oppression.

*O*ur government shouldn't make promises
we cannot keep—but we must keep the promises
we've already made.

❖

*W*hat is required [is] . . . a recognition on the part of
every American that we have duties to ourselves, our
nation and the world.

❖

*T*hose brave Americans . . . have something to tell us,
just as the fallen heroes who lie in Arlington whisper
through the ages.

❖

*S*mall countries can play a pivotal role in world events.

We will make sure that our daughters have the same rights . . . and the same freedoms to pursue their dreams as our sons.

True peace is not just freedom from fear, but freedom from want.

Knowledge and understanding is essential to peace.

Peace with justice means extending a hand to those who reach for freedom, wherever they live.

*U*ltimately our strength is grounded in our people—individuals out there, striving, working, making things happen.

✷

*N*o man can take away the dignity and grace that God grants us.

✷

*W*ords alone cannot meet the needs of our people.

✷

*B*eing true to our founding documents does not require us to agree on every contour of life.

It's what we've always done in America—set our sights high for ourselves, but even higher for our children.

✦

Peace is not merely the absence of visible conflict.

✦

It is ultimately the faith and determination of the American people upon which this nation relies.

✦

We must accept the challenge that all of us in democratic governments face . . . to have an open debate about how we use our powers.

*A*mericans aren't looking for a handout.
   They just want to work.

✺

*G*od calls on us to shape an uncertain destiny.

✺

*O*ur . . . ideals still light the world, and we will not give
   them up for expediency's sake.

✺

*I*nstead of just throwing money at our problems,
      we'll try something new in Washington—
      we'll invest in what works.

*W*ithout wise leadership in Washington, even the best-run businesses cannot do as well as they might.

❖

*O*ur journey . . . has not been the path for the faint-hearted, for those that prefer leisure over work.

❖

*I*n this democracy, government is no distant object but is rather an expression of our common commitments to one another.

❖

*A*ll people yearn for certain things: the ability to speak your mind and have a say in how you are governed.

*L*et us reach for the world that ought
to be—that spark of the divine that
still stirs within each of our souls.

*W*hen nations and peoples allow themselves
to be defined by their differences, the gulf
between them widens.

*F*reedom is not given, it must be won, through
struggle and discipline, persistence and faith.

*O*ur strength abroad is anchored in our strength
here at home.

*I*t's not enough to trade a prison of powerlessness for the
pain of an empty stomach.

*A*merica and Islam . . . share common principles—
   principles of justice and progress; tolerance and
   the dignity of all human beings.

❂

*W*e know we can't power America's future on energy
   that's controlled by foreign dictators.

❂

*E*ach society must search for its own path,
   and no path is perfect.

❂

*T*hey're so strong and they're so decent,
   the American people.

As Commander-in-Chief, I have no greater responsibility than keeping this country safe.

❂

I believe the success of the American economy depends not on the efforts of government, but on . . . America's businesses.

❂

We want our children to live in an America . . . that isn't threatened by the destructive power of a warming planet.

❂

America moves forward only when we do so together.

*D*emocracy cannot be imposed on any nation from the outside.

✦

*T*here will be times when nations—acting individually or in concert—will find the use of force . . . morally justified.

✦

*C*hange has always been built on our willingness, We The People, to take on the mantle of citizenship.

✦

*P*rogress . . . does require us to act in our time.

*W*e cannot afford half-measures, and we cannot go back to the kind of risk-taking that leads to bubbles that inevitably burst.

*J*ustice isn't about some abstract legal theory . . . . It's about how our laws affect the daily lives . . . of people.

*P*eaceful protest [can] shake the foundations of an empire and expose the emptiness of an ideology.

*W*ith common effort and common purpose, with passion and dedication, let us answer the call of history.

*I*n moments of trial and moments of
hardship . . . Americans rediscover
the ingenuity and resilience that
makes us who we are.

We, the people, understand that our country cannot succeed when a shrinking few do very well and a growing many barely make it.

✦

Let's not make the perfect the enemy of the essential.

✦

There are certain things we can only do together. There are certain things only a union can do.

✦

It is . . . undeniable that the Palestinian people— Muslims and Christians—have suffered in pursuit of a homeland.

*L*et us bridge our divisions . . . accept our responsibility
   to leave this world more prosperous and more
   peaceful than we found it.

✹

*S*anctions must exact a real price.

✹

*O*ur journey has never been one of shortcuts
   or settling for less.

✹

*N*o country will reach its potential unless it draws on the
   talents of our wives and our mothers, and our sisters
   and our daughters.

We believe in a generous America, in a compassionate America, in a tolerant America.

❊

The United States will stand up for [human rights] everywhere.

❊

The young are unconstrained by habits of fear, unconstrained by the conventions of what is.

❊

I know there's nothing weak—nothing passive— nothing naïve—in the creed and lives of Gandhi and [ML] King.

Inaction is not an option that is acceptable to me and it's certainly not acceptable to the American people.

Let us, each of us, now embrace with solemn duty and awesome joy what is our lasting birthright.

Freedom is a right for all people, no matter what side of a wall they live on, and no matter what they look like.

These are extraordinary times. For far too many Americans, the future is filled with unanswered questions.

War itself is never glorious,
and we must never trumpet it as such.

We do not have to live in an idealized world to still reach for those ideals that will make it a better place.

✷

Public service . . . ought to be about problem-solving and governance, not just how we can score political points.

✷

We can acknowledge that oppression will always be with us, and still strive for justice.

✷

It is entrepreneurship and industry that are the wellsprings of . . . the greatest force of progress and prosperity in human history.

*W*e can't delay and we can't go back to the same
worn-out ideas that led us here in the first place.

✦

I think that the more freely information flows,
the stronger the society becomes.

✦

*A*merica has never fought a war against a democracy . . .
our closest friends are governments that protect
the rights of citizens.

✦

*P*ublic service is a privilege.

The essential truth of democracy is that each nation
determines its own destiny.

✦

Our market has always been the engine
of America's success.

✦

We've all got to pull together and take our share of
responsibility. That's true here in Washington. That's
true on Wall Street.

✦

Tax cuts alone cannot solve all our economic problems.

What is required of us now is a new era
of responsibility.

✦

The starting point for our policies must always be
the safety of the American people.

✦

If you were successful, somebody along the line gave you
some help.

✦

While free markets are the key to our progress, they do
not give us free license to take whatever we can get.

*A*merica may have the strongest military in the world, but it must submit to civilian control.

❖

*W*e can always understand that most important decision—the decision we make when we find our common humanity in one another.

❖

*P*eace begins—not just in the plans of leaders, but in the hearts of people . . . in the daily connections.

❖

*L*ove and charity and duty and patriotism. That's what makes America great.

*I*t is inexcusable and irresponsible to get bogged down in distraction . . . while millions of Americans are being put out of work.

※

*T*he commitments we make to each other . . . do not make us a nation of takers; they free us to take risks.

※

A woman who is denied an education is denied equality.

※

*W*e are not as divided as our politics suggests. We're not as cynical as the pundits believe.

*I*f we are truly created equal, then surely the love we commit to one another must be equal as well.

*W*ith hope and virtue, let us brave once more the icy
currents, and endure what storms may come.

✺

I am convinced that in order to move forward,
we must say openly to each other the things
we hold in our hearts.

✺

*C*itizens. It's a word that doesn't just describe our
nationality or legal status . . . It describes what
we believe.

✺

*S*ocieties held together by fear and repression may offer
the illusion of stability . . . but they are built upon
fault lines.

You can't change Washington from the inside. You can only change it from the outside.

✺

We cannot depend on government alone to create jobs or economic growth. That is the role of the private sector.

✺

As a country, we will never tolerate our security being threatened, nor stand idly by when our people have been killed.

✺

That's where courage comes from—when we turn not from each other . . . but towards one another, and we find we do not walk alone.

*W*e can choose a world defined not by our differences, but by our common hopes.

❂

*T*here's a long history in this country of African-Americans and Latinos being stopped by law enforcement disproportionately.

❂

*D*on't stand idly by, don't be silent when dissidents elsewhere are imprisoned and protesters are beaten.

❂

*W*hile the future is unknowable, the winds always blow in the direction of human progress.

America is poised to lead the world once again toward new horizons.

⚙

When we welcome the immigrant with his talents or her dreams, we are renewed.

⚙

We must act, knowing that our work will be imperfect.

⚙

Those values upon which our success depends . . . have been the quiet force of progress throughout our history.

Capable, reliable, and transparent institutions . . . are the things that give life to democracy.

✴

We are made for this moment, and we will seize it— so long as we seize it together.

✴

Just and lasting peace cannot be measured only by agreements between nations.

✴

We will not cower in fear. We will not be intimidated. We will be vigilant. We will work together.

True progress is only possible where governments exist to serve their people, and not the other way around.

Standing still is not an option. It's not who we are; it's not who we have to be.

This is our first task as a society, keeping our children safe. This is how we will be judged.

Look, if you've been successful, you didn't get there on your own.

*C*hange does not come from Washington,
but to Washington.

*W*hile each of us will pursue our own individual
dreams . . . we rise or fall together as one nation.

❂

*I*t is easier to see what is different about someone than
to find the things we share.

❂

I believe that we must develop alternatives to violence
that are tough enough to actually change behavior.

❂

*A*merica has helped underwrite global security for more
than six decades with the blood of our citizens and
the strength of our arms.

A great nation must care for the vulnerable, and protect its people from life's worst hazards and misfortune.

The responsibility of improving this union remains the task of us all.

Real prosperity comes from our most precious resource—our people.

Every American will need to get more than a high school diploma.

Young people of every faith, in every country . . .
   have the ability to re-imagine the world,
   to remake this world.

America must play its role in ushering in
   a new era of peace.

Ideas cannot be contained by prison walls, or extinguished
   by a sniper's bullet.

The way to make government accountable is make it
   transparent.

The patriots of 1776 . . . gave to us a republic,
a government of, and by, and for the people,
entrusting each generation.

✺

Violence is a dead end. It is not how moral authority
is claimed; that is how it is surrendered.

✺

Growth can only be created if corruption is left behind.

✺

When we stand up for gay and lesbian brothers and
sisters, and treat their love and their rights equally . . .
we defend our own liberty.

Our common prosperity will be advanced by allowing all humanity—men and women—to reach their full potential.

✦

The presidency has a funny way of making a person feel the need to pray.

✦

We know our time on this Earth is fleeting.

✦

The strongest democracies . . . endure when people of every background and belief find a way to set aside smaller differences.

*T*his country only works when we accept certain obligations to one another and to future generations.

✪

*W*hen ordinary people have a say in their own future, then your land can't just be taken away from you.

✪

*P*eople in every country should be free to choose and live their faith based upon the persuasion of the mind, heart, and soul.

✪

A real recovery plan helps create more jobs and put people back to work.

*W*e lose ourselves when we compromise the very ideals that we fight to defend.

*S*o now it falls to us to seize the possibilities of this moment and convert peril into promise.

✸

*A*s soon as we're out of this recession, we've got to get serious about starting to live within our means.

✸

I want America's financial sector to be the most trusted and the most respected in the world. That requires reform.

✸

*W*e must confront [violence and injustice] not by splitting apart but by standing together as free nations, as free people.

*T*he way to make government responsible is
  to hold it accountable.

*W*e need to make the White House the people's house.

*R*esistance through violence and killing is wrong and
  does not succeed.

*O*nly by coming together . . . and expressing that sense
  of shared sacrifice . . . can we do the work that must
  be done.

*T*he role of citizen in our democracy does not end with your vote.

❂

*E*ven though we come from different places, we share common dreams.

❂

*O*nly a just peace based on the inherent rights and dignity of every individual can truly be lasting.

❂

*T*here are those who doubt whether true international cooperation is possible, given inevitable differences among nations.

*W*e always have the opportunity to choose
our better history.

❂

*M*y job is to solve problems, not to stand on the
sidelines and carp and gripe.

❂

*D*emocracy in a nation of 300 million can be noisy and
messy and complicated.

❂

*A*ll responsible nations must embrace the role
that militaries with a clear mandate can play
to keep the peace.

*N*o wall can stand against the yearnings for freedom, the
    yearnings for peace that burn in the human heart.

*W*e have the power to make the world we seek,
    but only if we have the courage to make
    a new beginning.

*P*eace in our time requires the constant advance
    of . . . tolerance and opportunity, human dignity
    and justice.

*W*e honor [brave Americans] not only because they are
    the guardians of our liberty but because they embody
    the spirit of service.

*P*eace is unstable where citizens are denied the right to speak freely or worship as they please.

✦

*T*here's no doubt that al Qaeda will continue to pursue attacks against us. We must remain vigilant at home and abroad.

✦

*O*ur own future is safer [and] brighter, if more of mankind can live with the bright light of freedom and dignity.

✦

*I*t is a sign of neither courage nor power to shoot rockets at sleeping children, or to blow up old women on a bus.

*W*e must begin by acknowledging the hard truth: We will not eradicate violent conflict in our lifetimes.

*T*o denounce or shrug off a call for cooperation is
an easy but also a cowardly thing to do.
That's how wars begin.

*W*e are true to our creed when a little girl born into
the bleakest poverty knows that she has the same
chance to succeed.

*S*ecurity does not exist where human beings do not have
access to enough food or clean water or the medicine
and shelter they need.

*T*he world has changed, and we must change with it.

*N*either America's interests—nor the world's—are served by the denial of human aspirations.

✸

*M*indful of the risks and costs of military action, we are naturally reluctant to use force to solve the world's many challenges.

✸

*B*eing true to our founding documents does not mean we all define liberty in exactly the same way.

✸

*O*nly when Europe became free did it finally find peace.

We can no longer afford indifference to the suffering outside our borders.

✦

This is a moment of great change in America, a time for reinvigorating our democracy and remaking our country.

✦

In this new global economy, standing still is the surest way to end up falling behind.

✦

Moral leadership is more powerful than any weapon.

*T*he consequences of war are dire, the sacrifices
     immeasurable.

✦

*W*hile freedom is a gift from God, it must be secured
     by His people here on Earth.

✦

*O*ur challenges may be new. But those values upon
     which our success depends are old.

✦

*A*merica has carried on . . . because we have remained
     faithful to the ideals of our forebears and true to our
     founding documents.

*F*reedom of religion is central to the ability of peoples to
live together.

✦

*T*he nation cannot prosper long when it favors only
the prosperous.

*E*ven though I'm president of the United States, my
power is not limitless.

✦

*F*or all the power of militaries and governments,
it is citizens who choose whether to be defined
by a wall or . . . tear it down.

*T*rue opportunity cannot exist when people are
    imprisoned by sickness, or hunger, or darkness.

*E*qual pay is by no means just a women's issue—it's a
    family issue.

*T*he more that TV pundits reduce serious debates into
    silly arguments, and big issues into sound bites, our
    citizens turn away.

*W*e need not be defined by our differences. We can be
    defined by the common humanity that we share.

The terms of peace may be negotiated by political leaders, but the fate of peace is up to each of us.

⚜

As Americans, and as a nation, we will not be terrorized.

⚜

If you actually took the number of Muslim Americans, we'd be one of the largest Muslim countries in the world.

⚜

Societies and economies only advance as far as individuals are free to carry them forward.

As it has for more than two centuries, progress will come in fits and starts. It's not always a straight line.

✦

To brush aside America's responsibilities to our fellow human beings would have been a betrayal of who we are.

✦

With the stakes this high, we cannot afford to get trapped in the same old partisan gridlock.

✦

The combined trends of increased inequality and decreasing mobility pose a fundamental threat to the American Dream.

*F*orward.
  That's where we need to go.

You must trust others so that they may trust you.

✸

That's the promise of tomorrow—that in the face of impossible odds, people who love their country can change it.

✸

We will rebuild, we will recover, and the United States of America will emerge stronger than before.

✸

Bin Laden was not a Muslim leader; he was a mass murderer of Muslims.

I believe that we will succeed or we'll falter as one people.

✦

*K*now that America is a friend of each nation, and every man, woman and child who seeks a future of peace and dignity.

✦

*G*rowth is more fragile and recessions are more frequent in countries with greater inequality.

✦

*T*he future must not belong to those who slander the prophet of Islam.

We will not apologize for our way of life, nor will we waver in its defense.

✦

Now, more than ever, we must do things together, as one nation and one people.

✦

To secure the gains this country has made requires constant vigilance, not complacency.

✦

I wake up every single day asking myself what can I do to give people a fair shot at the American Dream.

*P*eace with justice begins with the example we set here at home.

*I*f we choose to be bound by the past, we will never move forward.

*T*he commitments we make to each other . . . do not sap our initiative, they strengthen us.

*O*ur ability to influence others depends on our willingness to lead and meet our obligations.

*T*ogether. As one nation. As one people. That's how we
will beat back our present dangers.

❂

*W*e have inherited an economic crisis as deep and as
dire as any since the Great Depression.

❂

I am confident that if we can rise above these failures of
the past, then . . . we're going to emerge stronger
than before.

❂

*T*he strongest democracies flourish from frequent and
lively debate.

*W*e will defend our people and uphold our values through strength of arms and rule of law.

✵

*E*ach time we gather to inaugurate a President we bear witness to the enduring strength of our Constitution.

✵

*C*lear-eyed, we can understand that there will be war, and still strive for peace . . . for that is the story of human progress.

✵

I believe . . . that the forces that divide us are not as strong as those that unite us.

*T*he absence of hope can rot a society from within.

*W*e have begun the essential work of keeping the American Dream alive in our time.

*T*o those who cling to power through corruption and the silencing of dissent, know that you are on the wrong side of history.

*I*t is America's workers and businesses that employ them that will determine our economic destiny.

*O*ur economy is badly weakened, a consequence of greed and irresponsibility on the part of some.

It remains the task of us all, as citizens . . . to be the authors of the next great chapter of our American story.

✦

We reject as false the choice between our safety and our ideals.

✦

Change has never been simple, or without controversy. Change depends on persistence. Change requires determination.

✦

All of us must recognize that education and innovation will be the currency of the 21st Century.

*P*eace with justice depends on our ability to sustain both the security of our societies and the openness that defines them.

I work for the American people, and I'm determined to bring the change that the people voted for.

*E*gyptians have inspired us, and they've done so by putting the lie to the idea that justice is best gained through violence.

*T*he patriots of 1776 did not fight to replace the tyranny of a king with the privileges of a few or the rule of a mob.

I know that a call to arms can stir the souls of men and women more than a call to lay them down.

D ecisions are upon us and we cannot afford delay.

W hen we respect the faiths practiced in our churches and synagogues, our mosques and our temples, we're more secure.

O ur economy will be stronger for generations to come if we commit ourselves today to the work that needs to be done.

*O*ur actions matter, and can bend history in the direction of justice.

❖

I firmly believe…that sunlight is the best disinfectant.

❖

*P*eace is the only path to true security. . . . And there is no question that the only path to peace is through negotiations.

❖

*C*oncentrated wealth at the top is less likely to result in the kind of broadly based consumer spending that drives our economy.

*I*f we want to succeed, we can't fall back on the stale debates and old divides that won't move us forward.

❂

*W*hat makes America exceptional . . . [is the] belief that our destiny is shared.

❂

*B*ad things happen, and we must guard against simple explanations in the aftermath.

❂

*P*rosperity—broad, shared, built on a thriving middle class—has always been the source of our progress at home.

Washington may not be ready to get serious about energy independence, but I am.

America and Islam are not exclusive, and need not be in competition.

Democracy, more than any other form of government, delivers for our citizens.

We know America can't out-compete the world tomorrow if our children are being out-educated today.

*T*his country only works when we accept our rights are
wrapped up in the rights of others.

❂

*H*istory is [not] on the side of . . . those who use coups
or change constitutions to stay in power.

❂

*A*merica holds within her the truth that regardless
of race, religion, or station in life, all of us share
common aspirations.

❂

*T*his is a strong, powerful country that we live in and our
people are incredibly resilient.

*W*e should choose the right path,
    not just the easy path.

*W*e all hope for the chance to live out our lives with some measure of happiness and fulfillment for ourselves and our families.

*B*usinessess . . . generate the jobs . . . and serve as the foundation on which the American people's lives and dreams depend.

*I*t is when we are in the deepest valley, when the climb is steepest, that Americans relearn how to take the mountaintop.

*P*eace requires responsibility. Peace entails sacrifice.

*W*e may not be able to stop all evil in the world, but I know that how we treat one another is entirely up to us.

✸

I know that restoring transparency is not only the surest way to achieve results, but also to earn back . . . trust in government.

✸

*T*here are those who hear talk of a world without nuclear weapons and doubt . . . it's worth setting a goal that seems impossible.

✸

*W*e're greater together than we are on our own.

As the world grows smaller, our common humanity shall reveal itself.

❂

I believe that for all our imperfections, we are full of decency and goodness.

❂

The challenges we face are not just American challenges, they are global challenges.

❂

We, too, must act on behalf of justice. We, too, must act on behalf of peace.

*W*e want our children to live in an America that isn't burdened by debt, that isn't weakened by inequality.

*A*s long as I hold this office, I will do whatever it takes to put this country back to work.

*P*eople of goodwill, regardless of party, are too plentiful for those with ill will to change history's currents.

*T*he success of our economy has always depended . . . on the reach of our prosperity.

The most important office in a democracy is the office of citizen—not President, not Speaker, but citizen.

Now is the time to confront our problems head-on and do what's necessary to solve them.

It's bad for business to pay somebody less because of their gender or their age or their race or their ethnicity.

You and I, as citizens, have the power to set this country's course.

What makes you a man isn't the ability to conceive a child; it's having the courage to raise one.

Part of what led our economy to this perilous moment was a sense of irresponsibility.

Democracy can only endure when it's bigger than just one person.

Suppressing ideas never succeeds in making them go away.

*W*e know that our patchwork heritage
is a strength, not a weakness.

*I*t's important for us to pause for a moment and make sure that we are talking . . . in a way that heals, not a way that wounds.

✺

*T*he greatest tribute that we can pay to those who came before us is by carrying on their work to pursue peace and justice.

✺

*E*xperience shows us that history is on the side of liberty.

✺

*T*he American people did not choose this fight. It came to our shores, and started with the senseless slaughter of our citizens.

*W*e can't just rebuild the economy to where it was.
We're going to have to rebuild it stronger
than before.

I've never believed that government can solve every
problem or should.

*H*uman destiny will be what we make of it.

*S*cripture tells us that there is evil in the world, and that
terrible things happen for reasons that defy human
understanding.

Let them say that this generation . . . of Americans rose to the moment and gave America a new birth of freedom and opportunity.

❁

No one has a greater stake in a peaceful world than its most powerful nation.

❁

I'm not interested in groupthink.

❁

Democracy is a little messier than alternative systems of government . . . because democracy allows everybody to have a voice.

*N*o wall can stand against the yearning of justice.

✦

*D*emocracy is not something that is static; it's something that we constantly have to work on.

✦

I do not accept a United States of America that's second place.

✦

*T*he March on Washington . . . teaches us that the promise of this nation will only be kept when we work together.

You can make it here in America if you're willing to try.

America will remain the anchor of strong alliances in every corner of the globe.

The hard work of forging freedom and democracy is the task of a generation.

I have always believed that hope is that stubborn thing inside us that insists . . . that something better awaits us.

*T*he time for talk is over. The time for action is now, because . . . if we do not act, a bad situation will become worse.

*A*ll of us share this world for but a brief moment in time.

*W*e must accept the challenge that all of us in democratic governments face: to listen to the voices who disagree with us.

I got my start fighting for working families in the shadows of a shuttered steel plant.

*W*e cannot disguise hostility towards any religion behind the pretense of liberalism.

*W*e can no longer . . . consume the world's resources without regard to effect.

✦

*M*aking our economy work means making sure it works for everybody.

✦

*I*ntransigence must be met with increased pressure— and such pressure exists only when the world stands together as one.

✦

*F*or investment to lead to opportunity, reform must promote budgets that are transparent and industry that is privately owned.

*N*o human being can truly be imprisoned if hope burns in your heart.

✺

*O*n September 11, 2001, in our time of grief, the American people came together.

✺

*J*ust as past generations of Americans have done . . . we can and we must turn this moment of challenge into one of opportunity.

✺

*A*fter all of the politics and all of the posturing, this is about the right of every human being to live with dignity and security.

We will renew those institutions that extend our capacity to manage crisis abroad.

✦

Dr. King's . . . words belong to the ages, possessing a power and prophecy unmatched in our time.

✦

This is America. We don't disparage wealth . . . and we believe that success should be rewarded.

✦

Repression can take many forms, and too many nations . . . are plagued by problems that condemn their people to poverty.

*I*t's true that America cannot use our military wherever repression occurs.

❂

*N*o system of government can or should be imposed upon one nation by any other.

❂

*U*nlocking a nation's potential depends on empowering all its people, especially its young people.

❂

*F*or generations, the [USA] has played a unique role as an anchor of global security and as an advocate for human freedom.

We must act, knowing that today's victories will be only partial.

❂

Only a union could serve the hopes of every citizen to knock down the barriers to opportunity.

❂

All are equal, all are free, and all deserve a chance to pursue their full measure of happiness.

❂

Peace is unstable where citizens are denied the right to . . . choose their own leaders or assemble without fear.

Heroism does not require special training or
   physical strength.

✦

My fellow Americans, the oath I have sworn . . . was
   an oath to God and country, not party or faction.

✦

We are not a nation that leaves struggling families to
   fend for themselves.

✦

Let it be said by our children's children that we carried
   forth that great gift of freedom and delivered it safely.

We are the United States. There isn't any dream beyond our reach.

Whatever we think of the past, we must not be prisoners to it.

✦

You didn't send us to Washington because you were hoping for more of the same; you sent us there to change things.

✦

This is the moment for leadership that matches the great test of our times.

✦

It is that spirit, that innate longing for justice and equality, for freedom and solidarity . . . that can light the way forward.

Voting's the best revenge.

⊛

Progress does not compel us to settle centuries-long debates about the role of government for all time.

⊛

We cannot tolerate business as usual—not in Washington, not in our state capitols, not in America's cities and towns.

⊛

The end of the war in Iraq will enable a new era of American leadership and engagement in the Middle East.

*H*uman progress cannot be denied.

*T*his crisis has been a long time in the making. We're not going to turn it around overnight.

*F*or generations, we have done the hard work of protecting our own people, as well as millions around the globe.

*G*overnment can't light a spark in the mind of an engineer, but it can help an engineering student get loans to pay . . . tuition.

*I*am convinced that our daughters can contribute just as
much to society as our sons.

*T*he very idea at the heart of this country [is] that each
generation has a responsibility . . . for the next.

*A*s Americans, we all share the same proud title—
we are citizens.

*E*ven as we make difficult decisions about going to war,
we must also think clearly about how we fight it.

If we want a lasting peace, then the words of the international community must mean something.

America can do whatever we set our mind to.

The March on Washington teaches us that we are not trapped by the mistakes of history; that we are masters of our fate.

The interests we share as human beings are far more powerful than the forces that drive us apart.

*F*reedom is not an abstract idea; freedom is the very thing that makes human progress possible.

✺

*W*e, the people, still believe that every citizen deserves a basic measure of security and dignity.

✺

*A*frica doesn't need strong men; it needs strong institutions.

✺

I can report to the American people and to the world that the [USA] has conducted an operation that killed Osama bin Laden.

*O*ur problems must be dealt with through partnership; progress must be shared.

*A*merica's prosperity has always rested on how well we educate our children.

*F*reedom cannot exist when people are imprisoned for their political views.

*T*his administration stands on the side not of those who seek to withhold information, but those who seek to make it known.

*A*ll governments must maintain power through consent, not coercion.

❂

*W*e, the people, still believe that our obligations as Americans are not just to ourselves, but to all posterity.

❂

*A*s we speak, people in distant nations are risking their lives . . . just for a chance to argue about the issues that matter.

❂

*F*idelity to our founding principles requires new responses to new challenges.

*I*t always seems impossible until it is done.

We must try as best we can . . . so that human rights and dignity are advanced over time.

☀

Let us honor our past by reaching for a better future.

☀

We possess . . . youth and drive; diversity and openness; an endless capacity for risk and a gift for reinvention.

☀

The freedom which so many Americans have fought for and died for comes with responsibilities as well as rights.

*B*ecause of the drive and skill and talents of our people,
I believe . . . that our best days are still ahead of us.

✦

*P*olitics has to stop and we've got to get the job done.

✦

*S*ervice does not end with the person wearing the
uniform.

✦

*A*merica respects the right of all peaceful and law-
abiding voices to be heard around the world, even if
we disagree with them.

Around the world governments have an obligation to respond to their citizens.

❖

Complacency is not the character of great nations.

❖

Governments that respect the will of their own people, that govern by consent, and not coercion, are more successful.

❖

The American people have worked too hard, for too long, rebuilding from one crisis to see their elected officials cause another.

*R*ight now, we have a once-in-a-generation chance to act boldly, to turn adversity into opportunity.

*T*his cycle of suspicion and discord must end.

*S*ocieties based upon democracy and openness and the dignity of the individual will ultimately be more stable.

*A*merica's possibilities are limitless, for we possess all the qualities that this world without boundaries demands.

*P*art of the price of our own freedom is standing up for the freedom of others.

When it comes to rebuilding our economy, we don't have a moment to spare.

Evil does exist in the world. A non-violent movement could not have halted Hitler's armies.

Action and ideas are not enough. No matter how right, they must be chiseled into law and institutions.

The greatest nation on Earth cannot keep conducting its business by drifting from one manufactured crisis to the next.

We know education is the single best bet we can make to change the odds of our children and our cities.

✦

Each nation gives life to democracy in its own way and in line with its own traditions.

✦

The strongest foundation for human progress lies in open economies, open societies, and open governments.

✦

Aligning our reality with our ideals often requires the speaking of uncomfortable truths.

To say that force may sometimes be necessary is not a call to cynicism—it is a recognition of history.

In America, our destiny isn't written for us but by us.

To those leaders around the globe who seek to sow conflict . . . know that your people will judge you.

Public service is, simply and absolutely, about advancing the interests of Americans.

I do hope that we can all put politics aside and do the
American people's business right now.

✦

*W*e want our kids to grow up in a country where they
have access to the best schools and the best teachers.

✦

*D*emocracy is the most effective form of government
ever devised for delivering progress and opportunity
and prosperity and freedom.

✦

*N*o process of reform will succeed without national
reconciliation.

We do not believe that in this country freedom is reserved for the lucky, or happiness for the few.

❁

The private sector is doing fine.

❁

You don't like a particular policy or a particular president? Then argue for your position. Go out there and win an election.

❁

America does not presume to know what is best for everyone.

*W*e are stronger when all our people . . . are granted opportunity.

✦

*A*ll of us—we should do everything we can to make sure this country lives up to our children's expectations.

✦

*O*ur journey is not complete until all our children know that they are cared for and cherished and always safe from harm.

✦

*W*hat makes America exceptional are the bonds that hold together the most diverse nation on earth.

I face the world as it is, and cannot stand idle in the face of threats to the American people.

A country's greatest resource is its people.

✦

*W*e have chosen hope over fear, unity of purpose over conflict and discord.

✦

*N*o development strategy can be based only upon what comes out of the ground.

✦

*P*eace is . . . about breaking down the divisions that we create for ourselves in our own minds and our own hearts.

✦

There are no second-class citizens in our workplaces.

❂

For all the cruelty and hardship of our world, we are not mere prisoners of fate.

❂

Power comes from appealing to people's hopes, not people's fears.

❂

If you're willing to work hard, it doesn't matter who you are or where you come from or what you look like or where you [live].

❂

*F*ear is the force that stands between
human beings and their dreams.

We are an American family and we rise or fall together as one nation and as one people.

＊

When we fail to pursue peace, then it stays forever beyond our grasp.

＊

I know the road will be long, but I know we can get there.

＊

The American people . . . sent us here with a mandate for change, and the expectation that we would act.

*P*ublic service . . . ought to be more than just doing
what's popular in the moment.

✦

*W*e know from our own histories that intolerance
breeds injustice.

✦

*N*o person wants to live in a society where the rule of
law gives way to the rule of brutality and bribery.

✦

*S*o long as our relationship is defined by our differences,
we will empower those who sow hatred rather
than peace.

I respect those women who choose to live their lives in traditional roles. But it should be their choice.

✺

*H*ere in America . . . we've held fast to a vision of a better future, and we've been willing to work for it.

✺

*Y*ou and I, as citizens, have the obligation to shape the debates of our time.

✺

*T*hreats to freedom don't merely come from the outside. They can emerge from within—from our own fears, from disengagement.

In an era when our destiny is shared, power is no longer a
zero sum game.

✧

We share common dreams: to choose our leaders; to
live together in peace; to get an education and make
a good living.

✧

We are greater than the sum of our individual
ambitions, and we remain more than a collection of
red states and blue states.

✧

Knee-jerk disdain for government cannot rebuild our
levees or our roads or our bridges.

*W*e can shape our future,

or let events shape it for us.

*I*n a decent society, there are certain obligations that are
         not subject to tradeoffs or negotiation.

*T*ogether, we must work towards a world where
         we are strengthened by our differences,
         and not defined by them.

*F*reedom of speech, freedom of worship, freedom
         from want, and freedom from fear . . . reinforce
         one another.

*H*eroism is found not only on the fields of battle.

*S*tudy not only those who you agree with, but also those who you don't agree with.

✦

*R*econciliation is not a matter of ignoring a cruel past, but a means of confronting it with inclusion and generosity and truth.

✦

*W*e cannot mistake absolutism for principle, or substitute spectacle for politics, or treat name-calling as reasoned debate.

✦

*I*t's easier to start wars than to end them.

*P*rosperity without freedom is just another form
    of poverty.

❈

*L*et us look to the future with . . . hope not only for our
    own country, but for all those yearning for freedom
    around the world.

❈

*T*hese tragedies must end. And to end them,
    we must change.

❈

*A*s the world grows smaller, you might think
    it would be easier for human beings to recognize
    how similar we are.

*W*e can choose a world defined not by conflict, but by peace and justice and opportunity.

✦

*W*here force is necessary, we have a moral and strategic interest in binding ourselves to certain rules of conduct. All of us in Washington must remember that we're here to work for the American people.

✦

*O*ur power alone cannot protect us, nor does it entitle us to do as we please.

✦

I can say with complete confidence that endless delay or paralysis in Washington will only bring deepening disaster.

*E*nduring security and lasting peace
do not require perpetual war.

A free market only thrives when there are rules to ensure competition and fair play.

There is one rule that lies at the heart of every religion: that we do unto others as we would have them do unto us.

*A*merica's never been about what can be done for us. It's about what can be done by us together.

*I*t has been the risk-takers, the doers . . . who have carried us up the path towards prosperity and freedom.

The arc of the moral universe may bend towards justice, but it doesn't bend on its own.

✴

I do not believe that women must make the same choices as men in order to be equal.

✴

I believe America's greatest strength has always been society . . . that values and rewards the ingenuity of people.

✴

Engagement can more durably lift suspicion and fear.

*F*or our American story is not—and has never been—
about things coming easy.

✺

*W*e find ourselves in a rare moment where the citizens of
our country are watching and waiting for us to lead.

✺

*I*n reaffirming the greatness of our nation we understand
that greatness is never a given. It must be earned.

www.ingramcontent.com/pod-product-compliance
Lightning Source LLC
Chambersburg PA
CBHW071859020426
42331CB00010B/2585